FIVE ABBA HITS

FOR SSA CHOIR WITH

PIANO ACCOMPANIMENT

Novello Publishing Limited
14-15 Berners Street,
London W1T 3LJ

This collection ©copyright 1999 Novello & Company Limited
Music setting by Andrew Shiels
Cover design by Miranda Harvey
Printed in the EU

Money, Money, Money

Words and music by **Benny Andersson & Bjorn Ulvaeus**
Arranged by **Ralph Allwood & Lora Sansun**

©Copyright 1976 by Union Songs AB, Stockholm for the World.
Bocu Music Limited, 1 Wyndham Yard, Wyndham Place, London W1 for Great Britain & Eire.
All Rights Reserved. International Copyright Secured.

work all night, I work all day to pay the bills I have to pay. ___ Ain't it sad, ___
man like that is hard to find, but I can't get him off my mind. ___ Ain't it sad, ___

Ooh   Aah   Ain't it sad, ___

Ooh   Aah   Ain't it sad, ___

___ and still there nev - er seems to be a sin - gle pen - ny left for me, ___
___ and if he hap - pens to be free I bet he would - n't fan - cy me, ___

Ah ___

Ah ___

would-n't have to work at all, I'd fool a-round and have a ball.___
win a for-tune in a game, my life would nev-er be the same.___

Ooh ___

Ooh ___

Ba - da ba-da ba-da-ba da Ah Oo - ah ___

Ba - da ba-da ba-da-da, Ba - da ba-da ba-da-ba da Mon - ey, mon - ey, mon-ey, Oo-ah ___

Ba - da ba-da ba-da-da, Ba - da ba-da ba-da-ba da Mon - ey, mon - ey, mon-ey, Oo - ah ___

7

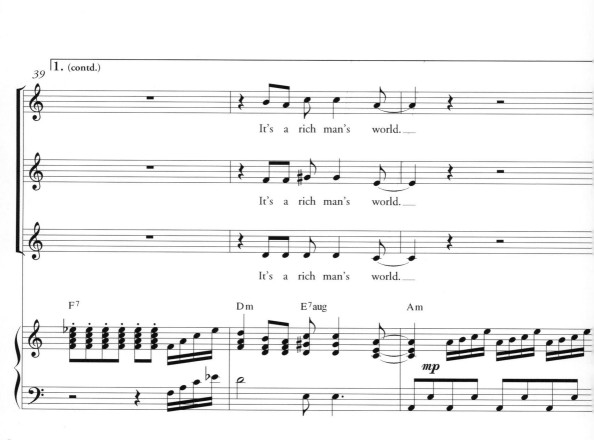

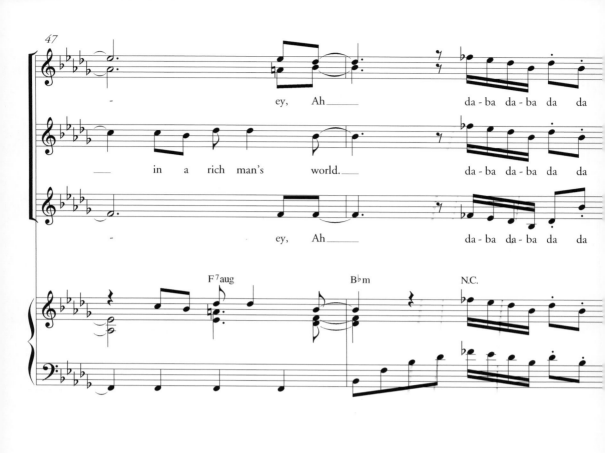

Dancing Queen

Words and music by **Benny Andersson, Stig Anderson & Bjorn Ulvaeus**
Arranged by **Ralph Allwood & Lora Sansun**

©Copyright 1976 by Union Songs AB, Stockholm for the World.
Bocu Music Limited, 1 Wyndham Yard, Wyndham Place, London W1 for Great Britain & Eire.
All Rights Reserved. International Copyright Secured.

19

dan-cing___ queen,___ yeh, yeh.   lights   are___ low,___ are low,

mf

Fri - day night___and the lights are low,___

dan-cing___ queen,___ yeh, yeh.   lights   are___ low,___ are low,

A   D/A   A   D/A

22

place to___ go,___   where they play___the right mu - sic,___

mp

place to___ go,___   where they play___the right mu - sic,___

mp

look - ing out___ for a place to go,___   Oh,___ where they play___the right mu - sic, ___

mp

A   F♯m   E   A/E

16

34

cresc.

mood for a dance,___ and when_ you get the___ chance,___

cresc.

mood for a dance,___ and when_ you get the___ chance,___

cresc.

mood for a dance,___ and when_ you get the___ chance,

F#m   E F#m   Bm⁷

37

f

___ you are_ the dan - cing___ queen,___ young and_ sweet,_ on - ly

f

___ you are_ the dan - cing___ queen,___ young and_ sweet,_ on - ly

f

___ you are_ the dan - cing___ queen,___ young and_ sweet_ on - ly

E⁷   A   D/A

Knowing Me, Knowing You

Words and music by **Benny Andersson, Stig Anderson & Bjorn Ulvaeus**
Arranged by **Ralph Allwood & Lora Sansun**

Soprano:
No more care - free laugh - ter,
Mem' - ries, good days, bad days,

Soprano 2:
No more care - free laugh - ter,
Mem' - ries, good days, bad days,

Alto:
No more care - free laugh - ter,
Mem' - ries, good - days, bad days,

©Copyright 1976 by Union Songs AB, Stockholm for the World.
Bocu Music Limited, 1 Wyndham Yard, Wyndham Place, London W1 for Great Britain & Eire.
All Rights Reserved. International Copyright Secured.

Know-ing me know-ing you, there is no-thing we can do.

Know-ing me know-ing you, Ah ha there is no-thing we can do.

bye. Know-ing me, know-ing you, Ah ha there is no-thing we can do.
say.

Dm   B♭7   C

Know-ing me, know-ing you, we just have to face it, this time

Know-ing me, know-ing you, Ah ha we just have to face it, this time

Know-ing me, know-ing you, Ah ha we just have to face it, this time

F   B♭ C

Chiquitita

Words and music by **Benny Andersson & Bjorn Ulvaeus**
Arranged by **Ralph Allwood & Lora Sansun**

©Copyright 1979 Music for UNICEF.
Bocu Music Limited, 1 Wyndham Yard, Wyndham Place, London W1.
All Rights Reserved. International Copyright Secured.

your own sor - row,

in _____ your eyes there is no hope for to - mor - row.

Sop. 1

mp

How I hate to see you like

Sop. 2

for to - mor - row.

mp

How I hate to see you like

sad, so qui - et._____ 2. Chi - qui - ti - ta, tell me the

sad, so qui - et._____ 2. Chi - qui - ti - ta, tell me the

Verse 2 & 3

truth,
down,

I'm a shoul - der
and your love's a

truth,
down,

I'm a shoul - der
and your love's a

Chi - qui - ti - ta,

34

bro - ken a feath - er,_____
you can de - ny it,_____

bro - ken a feath - er,_____
you can de - ny it,_____

bro - ken a feath - er,_____
you can de - ny it,_____

F♯m(add⁹)

36

mp cresc.

I_____ hope we can patch it
I_____ see that you're, oh, so

mp cresc.

I_____ hope we can patch it
I_____ see that you're, oh, so

mp cresc.

I_____ hope we can patch it
I_____ see that you're, oh, so

A   G   A   3   A⁷

up to - geth - er.___ / sad, so qui - et.___

Chi - qui - ti - ta you and I___

up to - geth - er.___ / sad, so qui - et.___

Chi - qui - ti - ta you and I___

up to - geth - er.___ / sad, so qui - et.___

D

(LH)

know

how the heart - aches come and they go and the

know

how the heart - aches come and they go and the

heart

G

time for griev - in'._____ Chi - qui - ti - ta you and I_____

time for griev - in'._____ Chi - qui - ti - ta you and I_____

time for griev - in'._____

cry but the sun is still in the__ sky and

cry you and I__ cry but the sun is still in the sky and

you and I__ cry but the sun is still in the sky and

⊕ CODA

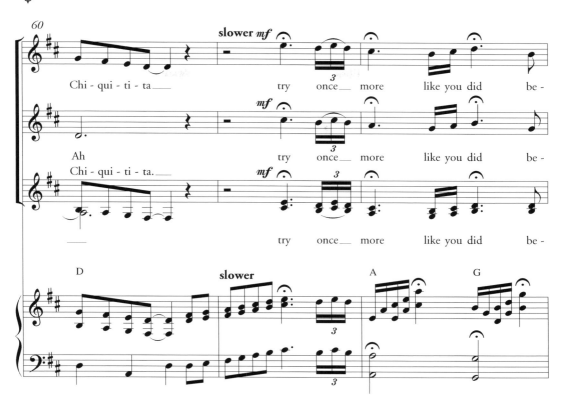

Mamma Mia

Words and music by **Benny Andersson, Stig Anderson & Bjorn Ulvaeus**
Arranged by **Ralph Allwood & Lora Sansun**

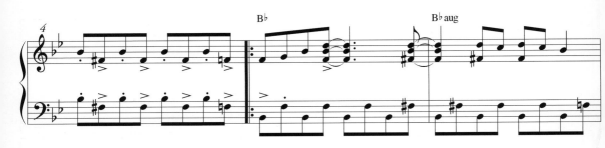

©Copyright 1975 by Union Songs AB, Stockholm for the World.
Bocu Music Limited, 1 Wyndham Yard, Wyndham Place, London W1 for Great Britain & Eire.
All Rights Reserved. International Copyright Secured.

45

46

48

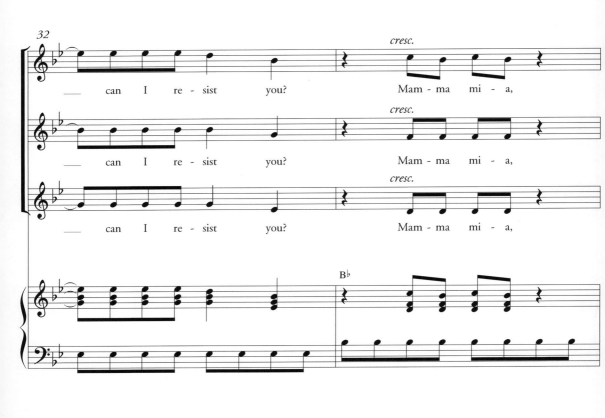

can I re - sist you? Mam - ma mi - a,

can I re - sist you? Mam - ma mi - a,

can I re - sist you? Mam - ma mi - a,

does it show a - gain, my, my, just

does it show a - gain, my, my, just

does it show a - gain, my, my, just

how much I've missed you? Yes,___ I've been bro - ken heart - ed,

how much I've missed you? Yes,___ I've been bro - ken heart - ed,

how much I've missed you? Yes,___ I've been bro - ken heart - ed,

blue___ since the day___ we part - ed, why, why did

blue___ since the day___ we part - ed, why, why did___

blue___ since the day___ we part - ed, why, why did___

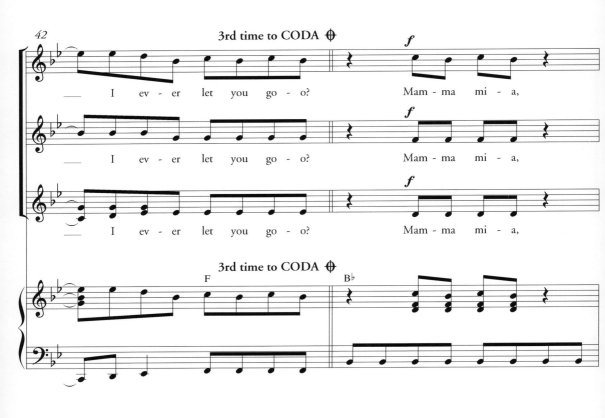

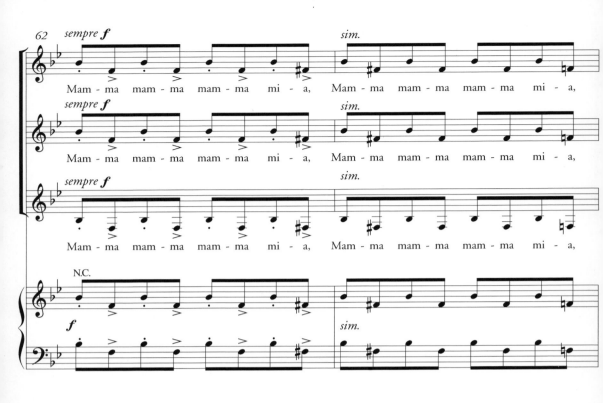

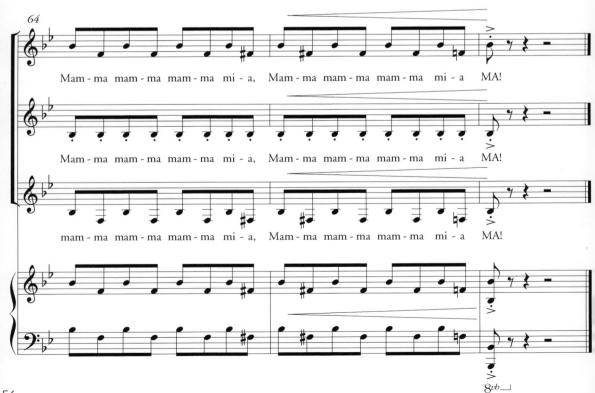

456789